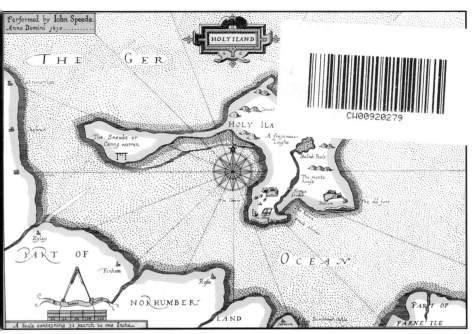

John Speede's map of Holy Island dated 1610

Lindisfarne, or Holy Island as we now know it, lies a few
hundred yards off the Northumbrian coast sixty miles north of Newcastle. Only
at high tide for about five hours is the island cut off from the mainland.

> For with the flow and ebb, its style
> Varies from continent to isle;
> Dry shod, o'er sands, twice every day,
> The pilgrims to the shrine find way;
> Twice every day the waves efface
> Of staves and sandalled feet the trace.

The island measures roughly a mile and a half from north to south and a
mile from east to west with a long narrow peninsula formed of sand dunes
stretching a mile and a half towards the mainland. In area it is 1,350 acres and
has a population of about one hundred and fifty mainly dependant on tourism,
shore fishing and farming. The rocks are limestone on the north and south
with sandstone on the east. Through these strata a mass of basalt called the
Lindisfarne Dyke has intruded forming the rock of Beblowe on which the castle

is perched, and the Heugh, a grassy cliff on which still stand the ruined walls of Fort Osborne (built in 1675) and the remains of a square structure called 'The Chapel'. The village lies beside the harbour and is made up of a few rows of old houses and squares built in typical Northumbrian style.

Below the Heugh is St Cuthbert's Isle on Hobthrush, a flat grass covered basaltic rock accessible at low tide. Here are traces of a little chapel called St Cuthbert in the Sea, which Bede says was used as a retreat by Cuthbert. In early times a lamp was kept burning here during the night to guide seamen into the harbour. The site of the altar is now marked by a stone cross.

Near the castle are the old lime kilns and the remains of a wooden jetty where the lime was loaded for transport to Scotland. The lime was quarried on the north of the island and brought by a railway, of which the embankment still stands, to the kilns below Beblowe. The main farm is St Coomb's situated a short distance north of the village. The name clearly suggests some association with St Columba but that a church in his name once stood here is doubtful.

Before the 11th century Holy Island was known as Lindisfarne. An early writer says the name was derived from a small stream called the Lindis which only appeared at low tide. This stream could possibly be identified with the Low which has to be crossed to reach the island today. The ending 'farne', also found in Farne Island, is from a Celtic word meaning land. Lindisfarne is therefore one of the rare Celtic place names of Northumberland.

The approach to Holy Island used to be rather difficult. There were two routes clearly marked by poles across the sands. The Pilgrims Way led direct for almost three miles from Beal Shore to Chare Ends crossing the stream called the Low.

On this track were 270 poles with two refuge boxes in case the traveller was trapped by the tide. The other route went direct to the Snook and then skirted the island until it likewise ended at Chare Ends. This was the route normally taken by the pony carts and battered old taxis, once familiar features of Holy Island life. Today a causeway makes it easy for motorists to cross the Low and the sands, and has opened the island to thousands of visitors who pass over when tides are suitable.

First Settlement

The history of Holy Island starts with the mission of Aidan in 634. Oswald had just made himself king of Northumberland by his victory over the Welsh prince Cadwallader at the battle of Heavenfield near the Roman Wall. Being a Christian he wished his people to accept the new religion and forsake their old pagan customs. To bring about this change he sent to Iona for Christian teachers. The first missionaries failed and returned home but they were replaced by Aidan and a group of Irish monks who settled at Lindisfarne because it reminded them of their island home at Iona and was close to the royal city of Bamburgh.

Here they established a monastic community which lived an austere and ascetic life as was usual in the Celtic church. Their monastery was a mere stockaded enclosure with a collection of primitive huts and a small oratory. From here Aidan evangelised the whole of Northumbria. He was the first of sixteen bishops of Lindisfarne. Of these the most famous was Cuthbert, the shepherd boy from the Lammermuir Hills. Cuthbert was born about 635 and entered the monastery of Melrose in 651, the year of Aidan's death. Here he served under Eata one of the twelve English disciples of Aidan. With Eata he went to Ripon and finally to Lindisfarne. Here he spent a great deal of his time as a hermit on Hobthrush. However, thinking it was not remote enough, he retired in 676 to a cell on Farne Island. His home was a circular cabin made of unhewn stone and turf and thatched with timber and bents. His food he produced on a plot of land nearby. For nine years he lived a life of prayer and contemplation on Farne Island.

In 685 Cuthbert was visited by King Egfrid who asked him to become Bishop of Lindisfarne. Reluctantly he consented, but within two years returned to his island retreat where he died in 687.

His body was brought from the Farnes to Lindisfarne where it was laid in a stone coffin on the south side of the altar. His fame brought many pilgrims to the church and in 698 his body was exhumed and placed in a wooden coffin which is still preserved at Durham. Above and inside this coffin relics were placed. When it was opened in 1104 a 6th century manuscript of St John's Gospel was found, a book probably belonging to St Cuthbert himself. The leather covering with its Celtic ornamentation is a unique example of early English leathercraft.

In 1827 the coffin was opened once again and further relics of St Cuthbert came to light, namely his comb, a small Pectoral Cross of gold, probably of 4th century workmanship, and a portable altar of embossed silver used by him on his journeys. Also discovered were richly embroidered vestments presented to the shrine of St Cuthbert in the 10th century.

During the Middle Ages St Cuthbert's remains lay in a rich shrine at the east end of Durham Cathedral. This shrine was destroyed at the Reformation but the coffin was reburied on the same site. Today the spot is marked by a stone in the floor inscribed with the name CUTHBERTUS.

Of the early Anglican monastery at Lindisfarne nothing survives save the collection of inscribed stones to be seen in the Priory Museum. Of these the greatest treasure is an early round-headed tombstone. On one side is depicted a band of armed Northumbrians brandishing swords and battle axes and wearing pleated kilts. On the other are two figures kneeling before the Cross with the sun and moon above. This stone is supposed to depict the Northumbrians before and after their conversion to Christianity. The existence of the sun and moon along with the cross shows how pagan ideas were incorporated into Christianity.

St Aidan's statue

There is also a fine collection of rare pillow stones, erroneously so-called because it was thought they were placed beneath the heads of corpses in Anglian times. Actually they were laid flat on the surface of the grave. They are small and inscribed on the side which lay uppermost with a cross very similar to those on the cruciform pages of the Lindisfarne Gospels. Above the arms of the cross the name of the person is written in runes, and below in Hiberno-Saxon letters. On one stone is a woman's name, Osgyth. The community at Lindisfarne in later years included many who were married and with children. Celibacy was clearly not strictly enforced. Osgyth may have been the wife or daughter of one of the clergy. On another broken stone are the letters AYD and many historians have suggested

4

King Egfrid visits Cuthbert on Farne Island and asks him to accept the Bishopric of Lindisfarne.

this may have marked Aidan's grave.

Numerous other objects are to be seen in the museum, including many carved fragments of monumental crosses which were so frequent in Northumberland in Anglican times. There is a large collection of medieval pottery found on Holy Island on the priory site, and as a reminder of its military occupation a well preserved gambling stone probably used by the garrison in the 1600s.

For the century and a half after Aidan settled on the island, life was peaceful and increasingly prosperous. But in 793 the Vikings landed and plundered the church of its treasures of silver and gold and murdered several of the monks. From now on fear of attack was always in the background and when a new invasion threatened in 875 the monks decided to leave, taking with them St Cuthbert's coffin and several other precious relics, including the bones of St Aidan, the head of St Oswald and the Lindisfarne Gospels. After much wandering they settled in Chester-le-Street in 883 eventually moving to Durham in 995.

For nearly two hundred years Lindisfarne was abandoned and the church and monastery became a ruin. But in 1069 fear of William the Conqueror drove the monks to flee to the safety of Lindisfarne with their precious relics. They stayed there for almost a year until it was safe to return to Durham.

Lindisfarne Gospels

The finest surviving work of art from Holy Island is the beautiful Lindisfarne Gospels. This superbly illuminated manuscript is a product of the Celtic tradition modified and developed in the English monastery of Lindisfarne. The early history of the manuscript is known from a note at the end written when the monks who looked after it were settled at Chester-le-Street. Here is a translation by Sir George Warner: "Eadfrith, Bishop of the church of Lindisfarne, he at the first wrote this book for God and St Cuthbert and for all the saints in common that are in the island, and Ethilwald Bishop of those of Lindisfarne Island, bound and covered it outwardly as well as he could. And Billfrith the anchorite he wrought as a smith the ornaments that are on the outside and adorned it with gold and with gems, also with silver overgilded, a treasure without deceit. And Aldred, an unworthy and most miserable priest, with God's help and St Cuthbert's overglossed it in English…"

The book consists of the four Gospels according to St Jerome's version together with the Eusebian Canons and two Epistles. It is written on two hundred and fifty-eight pages of vellum measuring 34 cm by 25 cm [13½ by 9¾ inches], in double columns of twenty-four lines. Most of the pages are plain, apart from small decorated initials. The main illumination occurs at the beginning of each Gospel where there is a page of elaborate cruciform design, and a page of ornamented text in pure Celtic style, and a miniature of the Evangelist, based on Byzantine models. The cruciform pages are completely covered with an interlaced pattern of birds and animals of intricate design. The pages of ornamented text are the initial letters of the Gospel elaborately enlarged and the first few words on a smaller scale. The portraits of the Evangelists though primitive are unique amongst English paintings.

The Gospels were at Lindisfarne for almost two hundred years until the island was abandoned in 875. Legend says the book was nearly lost when an attempt was made to cross over into Ireland. Although unlikely the story is so well known that we give it here in the words of Symeon of Durham:

"In this storm while the ship was lying over on her side, a copy of the Gospels, adorned with gold and precious stones, fell overboard and sank into the depths of the sea. Accordingly after a little while, when they had in some degree recovered their senses and reflected who and where they were, they bend their knees and prostrate themselves at full length before the feet of the sacred body, asking pardon for their foolish venture. Then they seize the helm and turn the ship back to the shore and to their fellows, and immediately they arrive there without difficulty, the wind blowing astern. Amidst their

lamentations their pious patron came to their aid. For appearing in a vision to one of them, Hundred by name, he bade them seek, when the tide was low, for the manuscript which had fallen from the ship into the midst of the waves: for perchance, beyond the utmost they could hope, they would, by the mercy of God, find it. For the loss of that book too had afflicted them with the most profound grief. Accordingly they go to the sea and find that it had retired much further than it was accustomed; and after walking three miles or more they find the sacred manuscript of the Gospels itself, exhibiting all its outer splendour of jewels and gold and all the beauty of its pages and writing within, as though it had never been touched by water. Further the above-mentioned book is preserved to this day in this church of Durham, which is honoured by the possession of the holy father's body, and, as we said before, no sign of damage by water is visible in it."

After much wandering the monks settled at Chester-le-Street in 883 and remained there until 995. It was here that the monk Aldred translated the Latin text into the old Northumbrian dialect thus making it the earliest surviving English version of the Gospels. Aldred's translation can be seen in small letters under the Latin capitals. When the monks left Chester-le-Street they moved south into Yorkshire, finally returning to Durham where the book remained on the coffin of St Cuthbert in the church erected in his honour. It was at Durham in the 12th century but thereafter history is obscure. Conflicting records say it was both at Durham and Lindisfarne in the Middle Ages. When the monasteries were dissolved in the reign of Henry VIII its gold and jewelled cover was probably taken off and melted down. In the 17th century it was in the hands of Robert Bowyer, then Clerk of the Parliaments under James I. From him it passed to the noted collector Sir Robert Cotton whose library now forms part of the British Library.

[View an interactive version of the *Lindisfarne Gospels* in the Lindisfarne Heritage Centre.]

Lindisfarne Priory

In the year 1082 William Carileph, Bishop of Durham, converted the cathedral establishment on the island into a Benedictine monastery, and bestowed upon the prior the church of Lindisfarne. Within two years the name was changed to Holy Island. The monks did not found a new independent monastery but a branch house or cell tenanted by monks sent from Durham and ruled by priors who were under the prior of Durham. The priory remained in this subordinate position throughout its history. "The holy Isle which was a mother of all the religiouse places in that part of the realme, becoming a hand-mayde to Durham."

Most probably the priory church we see today was started in the second quarter of the 12th century. An old account says the builder was a monk named Edward "who erected upon the Island, in honour of St Cuthbert, a church new from its foundations, which he finished of square stone, with all the elegance of workmanship". However, it is probable that the present ruins stand on the site of Edward's slightly earlier church.

Here until the dissolution of the monastery lived five or six monks under the rule of a prior. As endowments they had the parish of Holy Island, the manors of Fenham and Shorewood, and numerous farms on the mainland. Besides the land which they worked directly with their serfs they drew large tithes, mainly in kind, from their extensive parish.

The history of the priory is uneventful. The holding of the church services and the administration of their estates wholly occupied the small body of monks. Study, educational work and artistic creation were lacking. For many years the priory hadn't even a Bible among their meagre supply of books. Assisted by their servants, usually about twelve in number, the monks passed a quiet and pleasant life untouched by the troubles which periodically engulfed Northumberland.

As a cell of Durham the monks returned an annual account to their mother church as well as occasional inventories of the priory and its possessions. These documents, which have survived, provide us with a detailed account of the priory during the Middle Ages. In the 12th century they started burning seaweed for kelp. In 1344 they began quarrying limestone on the island, starting an industry which was to last over 500 years. About thirty years later they built boats for fishing. In the meantime the monastery was slowly extended, and the domestic quarters steadily improved.

For fear of the Scots, fortifications were introduced although the priory was never attacked except on one occasion in 1326 when William de Prendergast and his Scottish borderers pillaged the bakehouse and brewhouse. Occasionally

Reconstruction by R.Neville Hadcock shows how Lindisfarne Priory may have appeared in the 15th century. Compare this with the plan on page 13.

however their estates on the mainland were looted. As the old place rhyme well puts it:

> From Goswick we've geese; from Cheswick we've cheese;
> From Buckton we've venison in store;
> From Swinhoe we've bacon, but the Scots hav it taken,
> And the Prior is longing for more.

Coal, probably mined in the island, was extensively used in the priory. In 1344 they used 57½ chaldrons of coal (a chaldron is from 1 to 2½ tons) in the brewhouse, limekiln, hall, prior's chamber, kitchen and infirmary. The monks had many fires including one in the cloisters granted by special dispensation from Durham. The iron fire grate was probably invented at Holy Island where we first hear of it in 1362.

In 1537 with the Dissolution of the Monasteries the priory was closed and the 59th prior pensioned off as Bishop of Berwick. The priory buildings were converted into military storehouses.

'Rainbow Arch'

Priory Ruins

There is a close similarity between the architecture of the priory church and that of Durham Cathedral. Today it stands as a magnificent ruin. The dark red stone, which has weathered beautifully, stands out against a background of sea and fields. One of the ribs of the central tower still stands forming the picturesque 'rainbow arch'.

The priory consists of a church, with a cloister on its south side, surrounded by monastic buildings and an outer court occupying low ground at the foot of the Heugh. The church was completed in the 12th century, the monastic buildings in the 13th and 14th centuries. The church is of a dark red sandstone, the other buildings of a grey stone.

Church

The west doorway of the Church through which we enter today was intended for ceremonial purposes. The normal entry to the priory was by the main gate in the outer court. The church was copied from Durham and is in the Romanesque style. It consists of nave, chancel and transepts, being cruciform in shape. The original chancel was small with an apse, the foundations of which remain within the walls of the square-ended presbytery which replaced it in the second half of the 12th century. The building was vaulted with stone and surmounted by three towers, one in the centre over the transept crossing and two at the west end. One of the ribs which supported the central tower still stands, a striking feature with its zig-zag moulding and popularly called the 'rainbow arch'. The piers of the nave are of similar design to those in Durham Cathedral. Here we have the same compound and cylindrical piers, the latter decorated with incised designs of zig-zag, diaper and fluting. Only the east end of the church was used by the monks, their choir occupying the transept crossing. They were separated from the nave by a stone screen or pulpitum, the marks of which can be seen in one of the piers. Between the next two piers was the rood-screen above which was a crucifix, known as the rood. Between the pulpitum and the rood-screen sat the aged and infirm members of the monastery. The nave was used for processions and on special occasions by the people of the village.

Cloisters

The cloisters were intended for study and contemplation and were used for processions. The cloister walks at Holy Island are incomplete and were really only covered passages leading to the various domestic buildings which surrounded the cloister. Here instead of a monastic plan we have domestic needs predominant.

Nave of the priory

Chapterhouse

On the east side of the cloister adjoining the south transept are the vestry and chapter house. The monks met each day in the chapter house where a chapter of the rules of St Benedict were read to them after the fourth service, Tierce, which was held sometime between 8-30 a.m. and 10-30 a.m. Formal meetings were also held here. On the first floor above was the monks' dormitory or dorter. It was a long building divided into cubicles, for all had to sleep in the same room, even the prior in early days. From the dormitory a night stair led into the church and a day stair into the parlour. Remains of both can be seen. During certain times of the day monastic rules enjoined silence. But if talking was essential at such times the parlour could be used. East of the chapter house and outside the walls was the monks' graveyard, now called the 'sanctuary-garth' in which there are several internments.

Prior's chamber

Next to the parlour is the common room with the prior's chamber above. The common room or warming-house was the only place excepting the kitchen where a fire was at first admitted. Originally the prior slept with the monks but as time went on he moved to an adjoining room. The priors' chamber was probably divided into a study and a bedroom with a private oratory on the same floor. Close by was the great chamber where important guests were accommodated. In the last inventory before the Dissolution we read that the prior's rooms were well furnished with two beds, two presses, two chests, one cupboard and a chair, and decorated with embroidered hangings and a tapestry. The bed in the great chamber had curtains of red saye and the walls were hung with red worsted.

Dining hall
Along the south side of the cloister was the monks' dining hall or refectory or frater. Near the middle are the remains of a hearth and in the south wall a windowsill is embedded with two sculptured faces supposed to depict a monk and a nun.

Kitchen etc.
The dining hall was divided from the kitchen by a wooden screen which formed a passage leading to the doorway by which the cloisters were entered from the outer court. The first two rooms were the kitchen and larder. In the latter is a stone-lined pit probably used as a refrigerator. Behind the larder is a room with a brick-lined oven but since there is no trace of a fireplace it was probably heated by a wood fire inside the oven. West of the kitchen is the bakehouse. Here on a platform is a brick-lined structure for a large boiler. Both these rooms have their original flooring. The next room is the brewhouse with a circular mash tub let into the floor and a sink, the leaden pipe from which can still be seen at the north end of the frater screens.

On the west of the cloister are three rooms. Two are cellars and the third a pantry or buttery. Originally they formed one large storehouse divided by wooden partitions. The stone dividing walls were added later. Above were

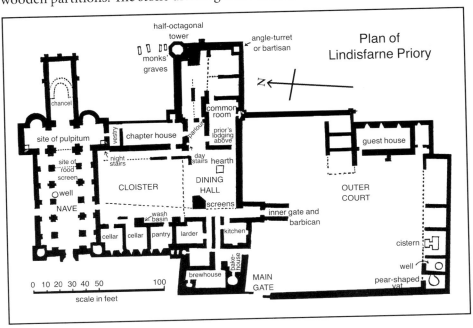

probably the servants' or lay brothers' quarters. In the alley in front is a trough or wash basin.

Outer courtyard In the Middle Ages the visitor entered the monastery by the main gate called in the records the 'yet-howse tower' which opened in to the outer court. This presented the appearance of a farm yard although today many of the buildings have disappeared. Along the west wall were probably wooden pent houses of which nothing remains. In the south-west corner are the remains of three rooms. Starting from the corner the first, with a cobbled floor, contains a pear-shaped vat, the second a well, and the third two cisterns communicating with each other by a channel passing through a small archway. The next two buildings were probably stables with storehouses above. Against the east wall are the ruins of what was probably the guest-house which was of two storeys. On the upper floor was the hall and chamber while the loops which can be seen lighted the cellar below. Next to the guest-house are three chambers, one paved and cobbled. They were possibly parts of the granary. The entrance from the outer court into the main buildings is by a gateway strengthened by a barbican in the 14th century. A barbican is an outer gate pushed forward for additional security. The barbican at Holy Island is unique for a monastery.

Fortifications Following the English defeat at Bannockburn, Northumberland was repeatedly raided by the Scots in the 14th century. Along with other northern monasteries Holy Island was fortified. Many traces of these fortifications survive. Along the west wall of the outer court can be seen the parapet walk and battlements. The strongest defences were to the east of the prior's apartments. The projecting series of chambers, which were probably the infirmary, were defended by very thick walls. At the south-east corner is an angle turret or bartizan corbelled out of the walls. Here legend says a nun was immured alive as punishment, a story originating from the story of *Constance of Beverley* as told by Scott in his poem *Marmion*. At the north-east corner was a half-octagonal tower, a massive building of which only the base has survived. In the 14th century the west front was heightened and crossbow loops added for additional security. Two of these loops can still be seen. The monastery would have been defended by the servants and in the inventories are frequent references to the arms they had.

In the 14th century the armour and weapons available were few. It was in 1348 that the monks started buying armour for their defence, but by 1362 there was only complete equipment for one man and limited armour for five others. In the 15th century the armour and weapons are more varied. In 1437 among a large military inventory appear 5 guns, while at the end of the century there are 10 stock guns and 5 large muskets, but only one crossbow. In 1346 when Northumberland was laid waste before the battle of Neville's Cross the prior paid a man sixpence a day to stand at the Snook End to warn of the approach of Scottish raiders.

Ornamented Norman doorway on west front of priory – engraving c.1840

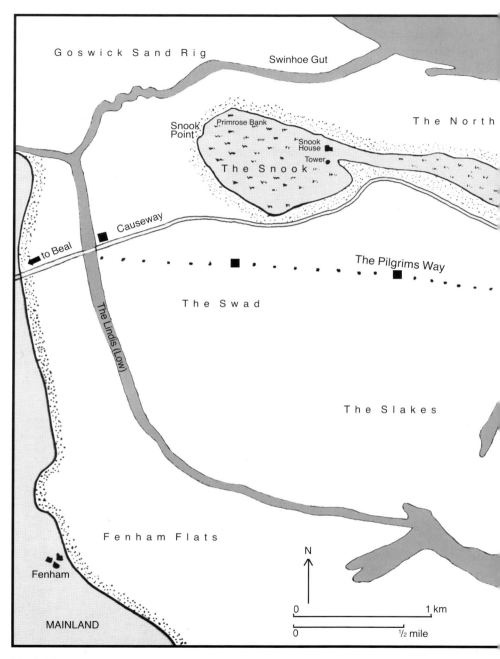

Goswick Sand Rig

Swinhoe Gut

The North

Snook Point

Primrose Bank

Snook House

Tower

The Snook

Causeway

to Beal

The Pilgrims Way

The Lindis (Low)

The Swad

The Slakes

Fenham Flats

Fenham

MAINLAND

N

0   1 km

0   ½ mile

The 'white' area and the causeway flood at high tide.
Safe-crossing timetables are located at both ends of the causeway.

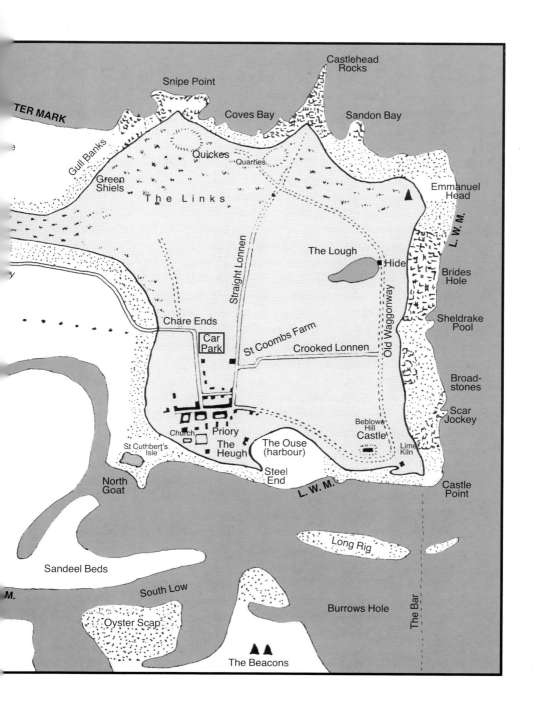

TER MARK

Snipe Point

Castlehead
Rocks

Coves Bay

Sandon Bay

Gull Banks

Green
Shiels

Quickes

Quarries

The Links

Emmanuel
Head

L. W. M.

Straight Lonnen

The Lough

Hide

Brides
Hole

Sheldrake
Pool

Chare Ends

Car
Park

St Coombs Farm

Crooked Lonnen

Old Waggonway

Broad-
stones

Scar
Jockey

Church

Priory

St Cuthbert's
Isle

The
Heugh

The Ouse
(harbour)

Beblowe
Hill
Castle

Lime
Kiln

North
Goat

Steel
End

L. W. M.

Castle
Point

Long Rig

Sandeel Beds

M.

South Low

Burrows Hole

The Bar

Oyster Scap

The Beacons

Island Life since 1537

With the closure of the priory a new chapter in Holy Island's history opens. The priory is soon being used as "the Queen's Majestie's storehouse", a castle has been built on Beblowe rock, and the island becomes an important naval base. The village however did not prosper. Still isolated and poverty stricken the islanders during the next three hundred years were notorious for their lawlessness.

Like so many Northumbrians in the coastal villages they became 'wreckers' and smugglers, and many fine ships were lured on to the dangerous rocks which abound near their island home. Father Blakhal, a Roman Catholic missionary, whose ship took refuge in Holy Island harbour during a storm in 1643, described how the minister of the parish and one of the local gentry fought for a box of castor hats with gold hat-bands which were washed up from a wreck "and the minister did sore wound the gentleman". The islanders' nefarious activities were confirmed by the governor, the famous Robin Rugg, who told Father Blakhal: "The common people ther do pray for shippes which they sie in danger. They al sit downe upon their knees and hold up their handes and say very devotedly, Lord, send her to us, God send her to us. Seeing them upon their knees, and their hands joyned, you do think that they are praying for your sauvetie; but their myndes are far from that. They pray, not God to sauve you, or send you to the port, but to send you to them by shipwrack, that they may gette the spoile of her. And, to show that this is their meaning, said he, if the shippe come wel to porte, or aschew naufrage, they gette up in anger, crying, the Devil stick her, she is away from us."

Before the Dissolution of the Monasteries the Bishop of Durham was the sole owner of Holy Island, and although some of the land was given to the priory the town itself remained in his possession and was administered by a bailiff. In 1559 the rights of the Bishop in Islandshire were taken over by the Crown and eventually came into private hands.

Part of the land in the 18th century was held in common and before the Enclosure Act of 1793 the following position prevailed according to an old document:

"The town of Holy Island is an ancient town, and the inhabitants are distinguished into burgesses as they are called in ancient writings, or freemen, and stallengers. The burgesses or freemen are those who have houses in the town called freehold houses in number twenty-four. The stallengers are the owners of the other houses. There are belonging to the freehold houses certain lands inclosed, as there are crofts and gardens belonging to the Stallengers' houses. The rest of the island (save the lord's pasture close) is a sandy soil whereon grows a sort of grass called bents, and is common among the freeman, who have each a right to depasture a certain number of cattle thereon, and to cut the bents for covering their houses, to dig in the freestone quarries for stones for their use, to keep a fishing boat for the catching of cod and other fish to cure and dry them on the common field, where there is a place made for the purpose, and to draw their boats for safety above the full sea mark, and lay them there on the said common. The stallengers have a right to depasture their cattle also, but they are stinted to a lesser number than the freemen are."

By the Bill for the Enclosing the Common Land of the Island passed in 1793 the following changes were made. The Lord of the Manor retained the right of hawking, hunting, fowling and fishing. But the freemen gave up their right of common and in return were granted small plots of land near the village. Jenny Bell's Well, Plopey Well, and Brigwell were made public. The freemen were still allowed to work the freestone and limestone quarries at the Coves in a fair and regular manner with the right of erecting one kiln for burning limestone.

Fishwives Old Sarah and Bessie Morris – based on a 19th century photograph

Land was set aside for a workhouse and school. The land between the Ouse and the Sanctuary Close was let to the fishermen for the purpose of their trade but the Heugh remained common. For one month late in the year the ancient right of gathering bent was still allowed. Among the names of the freeholders mentioned in the award are many families still resident on the island.

With the 19th century an era of prosperity dawned on the island. The main development was in herring fishing where the number of boats steadily increased. Most of the herring were cured for export to the Baltic. A former red brick curing house still stands on the green above the Ouse and a long building at the rear of the Iron Rails was used for the same purpose.

Iron Rails – once one of nine inns but now a private house

In the year 1859 when the herring fishing was at the height of its prosperity a well known traveller and writer, Walter White visited the island and made the following comments:

"While crossing the churchyard, we notice a remarkable contrast between the abodes of the living and the numerous large and ornamental gravestones and elaborate tombs, and you will perhaps think that the pains bestowed on memorials of the dead would be better employed within the village, or 'the

20

town' as the natives fondly call it. There is a square bestrewn with unsavoury rubbish, and the condition of the streets accords therewith, implying that public cleanliness has not yet grown into a habit. The spring is a good way off. Whitewashed cottages, some of them retaining the primitive thatch, constitute the bulk of the dwellings, while among those of better style appear nine inns or public-houses (The Ship Inn, the Fisherman's Arms, the Selby Arms, the Northumberland Arms, the Castle Hotel, the Britannia, The Plough Inn, the Crown and Anchor, and the Iron Rails). In the last census returns the population of the island is given as 908, of whom 458 are males; hence, excluding boys, we may form a notion as to the number of customers to each public house. It is said that if good lodgings were available, the island would be more visited than it is by sea-bathers; but the difficulty of access and the want of pleasant scenery are perhaps the chief reasons against immigration.

"We saw 'the town' under the busy aspect, preparing for the herring fishery; nets lay in heaps, or stretched out fifty or sixty yards, while men and boys disentangle their mazy folds and tie the loops; around almost every door lies a heap of floats, and lines, and queer-looking oil-skin garments, and ample sou'westers hang on the walls. And at times a few men, wearing thick sea-going jackets, and boots up to their hips, take their way down to the beach with a pile of gear on their shoulders. They will sail ere long, for rumour says the herring are in the offing.

Holy Island's village square or market place with the Celtic cross erected, in 1828, on the site of the old market cross

"The castle stands about half a mile eastward of the village. On our way thither, we passed the beach where the fishing-boats come in, and saw the huge wooden vat – if vat it be – round which the women stand to clean the herrings, and on the other side of the road fourteen hundred herring-barrels in piles and rows, and two men industrious over their final preparation."

There has always been lime quarrying on the island since the monks started the industry, but about 1850 a Dundee company began to develop the trade on a big scale. Lime-kilns, railways and jetties were built. Attempts were made to mine coal and ironstone near Snook House and a stone tower stands as a reminder of this short lived venture. New workmen were brought over from the mainland and the population began to grow reaching a record number of over 600. From 1850 the island also became a popular watering place with the local gentry, and a centre for shooting and fishing.

With the turn if the century this short lived prosperity was over. The herring fisheries vanished, the big boats were laid up to become cabins, and only inshore fishing chiefly for lobsters, remained. About the year 1900 the lime kilns closed. The population began to decline and the islanders came to depend more and more on the tourist trade.

The village square (or Market Place) is well laid out. The weekly market which was held here for centuries had by 1860 ceased to be of any importance and has long been discontinued. On the green is a Celtic cross which was designed by John Dobson and set up in 1828 on the site where the old market cross used to stand. The old stump was removed to a place near St Mary's Church where it is still used as part of a Holy Island wedding ceremony. It is called the Petting Stone, and it is the custom for brides to jump over it for luck, supported by two old fishermen. On one side of the square is the Manor House. It is one of the finest houses in the village and was probably built in the middle of the 19th century. Once, when the lime trade flourished there were nine inns of which two, the Crown and Anchor and The Ship, have survived. Now a private house, the Iron Rails owes its name to either the railings at the entrance or more probably to the railway which once ran near it, at the time when the lime trade was of importance.

The small streets and squares of Holy Island have very old names which remind us of the early history of the village. Although they are rarely used today here's a list the names found in the 19th century: Prior Rawe, Mary Gate, Piet Hill, North Street, Crossgate, Church Lane, Crosse Market, Palace Gate, Fenkle Street, Sea Sheite, Middle Sheite, Smales Garth, Comes Sheite, Broad Street, South Baggot, Baggot Heugh, Cuddys Walls, St Combs, Coldringham Walls.

Castle

The castle on Holy Island owes its existence to an Order in Council issued in 1539 ordaining that "all havens should be fensed with bulwarks and bloke houses against the Scots". In 1543, on the occasion of Lord Hertford's raid into Scotland 2,200 soldiers were landed on the island and ten line-of-battle ships anchored in the harbour. In 1548-9 King Edward VI engineers were ordered "to view the place by the church, what hill or grounds were mete for fortification there".

Building started immediately using stone from the ruined priory and in the Border Survey of 1550 it is mentioned as the "Fort of Beblowe which lyeth very well for the defense of the haven". The garrison was not large. In 1559 it consisted of a non-resident captain, two master gunners at 1s. per day, a master's mate at 10d. per day, and twenty soldiers at 8d. per day. A report made to the Crown in 1561 has some interesting information about the island and castle:

"The Holy Iland is scituate within the sea, and yit at every tyde of lowe water men may passe into the same on horseback or foote, and it is in compasse about iijor myles by estimat or more, and hath in the same a little borowgh towne all sett with fishers very poore, and is a merkett town on ye Satterday, howbeit, it is little vsed, and yit by reason thereof all the townes of Norham and Ilandshyre ought theire to receive yr measors and wights, and are in all things to be directed by thaisse of the said towne of Iland. And there was in the same Iland one Cell of Monks of the house of Durham, which house hath the personage of the said parish as before is declared, which mansione howse was built in fovre square of two Courts, as appeareth by the platt theirof, and nowse the same howse in the Quene's Maties storehouse and also another howse in the towne called Pallace, which is the newe brewhouse and bakehouse, and the other Offices in the same for the said storehouse. And in the same Iland is also one forte builded vpon an hill called Beblowe, which serveth very well for the defence and saveguard of the haven, the which haven is a very good and apt haven both of the harborowe and landinge. The inhabitants there have baylifs and all other officers of their owne elections yerely, charged at Michmas, and have certeine men which be burgesses and fremen, of wch companie the sayd officers be always chosen. And everye burgesse payeth certen burrowe rent, save xij or xiij, which clame to be free that they never payd anye burrowe fearme. The moreparte of the towne is nowe decayed in howses, and yit the tofts and crofts where the howses did stand remayne, of which the burrowe rent is nowe for the most part collected and raysed, as hereafter doth appeare."

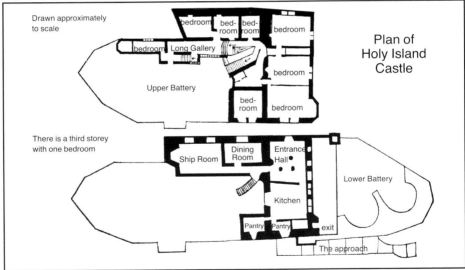

Although the castle lost its importance with the union of England and Scotland under James I it still remained a government fortress. John Aston who visited it in 1639 described it as a "pretty fort recently repaired and put into forme". There were two batteries and "on the lower stood mounted 3 iron peeces and 2 of brasse, with carriadges and platformes in good order. On the higher was one brasse gunne and two iron ones with all ammunition of them. There are 24 men and a captain kept in pay to man it, the common souldiours have 6d. per diem". The governor was Captain Rugg, described by another visitor as just as "famous for his generous and free entertainment of strangers, as for his great bottle nose, which is the largest I haven seen".

During the Civil War the castle came into the hands of the Parliamentary forces but its importance as a military base was over. Slowly it fell into decay although a garrison was maintained until 1820. It was then converted into a coastguard station and later became the headquarters of an Island detachment of the Northumberland Artillery Volunteers.

In 1903, Edward Hudson of *Country Life* magazine, on a visit to the island found the castle a ruin. With the aid of Sir Edwin Lutyens the famous architect he had the castle restored as a home to live in.

Kitchen

The castle now consists of two batteries, the lower facing south-east and the upper due south. The buildings form two blocks at right angles. The entry hall is completely modern and leads to two plain vaulted chambers known as the Dining Room and Ship Room. They were originally magazines and the original stonework and brick floors have not been greatly altered. On the second floor are bedrooms facing south and east. They are joined by a long gallery which reminds one of a ship's deck. The rooms are filled with a fine collection of antique furniture, mostly oak, of English or Flemish of the early 17th century. Ornaments and pictures are all in harmony making a unique and picturesque home. The castle and its contents were given to the National Trust in 1944 by Sir Edward de Stein and his sister Miss Gladys de Stein.

Dining Room of the castle

Parish Church

The parish church of St Mary lies immediately west of the priory and was built some time before 1145. For a long time it was the mother church of the district known as Islandshire which covered a considerable area on the mainland. On the outside the dominating feature is the 18th century bell-cote, resting on two large buttresses which are joined high up by an arch. The interior is rather complicated. In the west front can be seen some crude masonry which probably belongs to the original structure. The three eastern arches separating the nave from the north aisle may also belong to this early building. They are certainly Norman work, being round-headed resting on cylindrical and unornamented columns of red stone. The chamfered ribs of the arch are built of alternative red and white stones, the only Northumbrian example of such ornamental treatment. The fourth arch of the north aisle is pointed, and was probably built shortly after the three Norman arches, being in the early English style. The north aisle is called the Haggerston aisle, because it was for a long time the burial place of that family. It is lighted by three windows, two in the north and one in the eastern wall. They are all under pointed arches, the one in the east being of three lights with plain tracery, and those on the north of two. All are probably of early 15th century date and in the Decorated style.

The south arcade is of the early English character and was built in the 13th century. The arches are pointed, resting on octagonal piers with plain capitals. The original windows were removed at an early period and replaced by two in the decorated style. In the west wall are three long lancet windows, one from the nave and one from each side aisle.

The chancel is also early English, and is lighted by eight lancet headed windows. Here are two old aumbries and a medieval tombstone carved with a cross, sword and mitre-shaped shield. Near the chancel arch is the tombstone of Sir William Reed of Fenham who died in 1604. On it is the curious inscription, *Contra vim mortis non est medicamen in hortis.* (Against the power of death there is no remedy in the garden). The parish registers commence with the end of the 16th century and have many interesting entries.

Monastic Records

We have already mentioned the accounts and inventories of the Prior which have survived from the Middle Ages. They give an intimate picture of the way in which the monastery was conducted. We have made a selection from the expenditure incurred during the 14th century to illustrate aspects of monastic life not already mentioned. The original records are in Latin and the translation is by the Reverend James Raine who, in the 19th century, wrote a notable history of Holy Island.

Two pounds of sugar of Cyprus, 16d. Two boxes of ginger, 20d. Four pounds of saffron, 8lbs of pepper, 60lbs of almonds, 16lbs of rice, 7 flaggons of oil olive, and one basket of figs, £4.

To Gilbert de Trewyk, to put him to school, and to Robert de Trewyk for medical attendance on the Prior and cell, 34s.

Woollen cloth, to make robes for six esquires, and two clerks, with furs and dressing, and for nine servants and 3 boys without fur, £9 11s. 8d.

Ninety ells of linen cloth and 14 pieces of linsey-woolsey, bought for the Monks, 39s. 7d.

Wine bought for the Communion of the parishioners in the Monastery and Chapels, 52s 8d.

Timber bought for the new chamber of the Prior, 26s. 2d.

To master John the Carpenter, in full, for building the great chamber, 26s. 8d.

To John Grubber, for covering the Grange and the long stable, 16d.

To William Smith, for sharpening the tools of the masons, 2s.

Sixty-nine horse shoes and 56 removes for the palfreys, back carriers and hackneys.

To William the Smith, for mending the bends of the great and inner gate, and for repairing divers winders within the court, 2s. 5d.

To William the Mason, for 57 weeks, 43s. 10d.

To the same, as an allowance for his robe, 8s.

To Thomas de Ellwyk, the mason, for his shoes, 3s. 4d.

To John the Clerk, for shaving the monks for a year, 4s.

Fifty-six pounds of candles of Paris for the hall and chamber, bought at Berwick and Bamburgh, per lb.1½d - 5s. 10d.

To Alice de Ekeles, for divers necessaries, and to two women who milked the sheep, 16d.

To the common cowherd, for watching the Priors' cows, 3d.

Gloves for 14 servants when they gathered the tythe corn, 2s. 8d.

One long settle or seat for the hall, and repairing the cushions, 3s. 10d.

Two pairs of boots bought for the Prior, 5s.

His expenses at the funeral of the Lady Ada de Manners, with six pairs of gloves bought, 2s. 2d. Twelve pairs of gloves bought for the Prior, 18d.

To the Skinner, for repairing the fur of the Prior's hoods and tunics, 14d.

Bought 2½lb. of draget - 1 quarteron of cloves - half a pound of white pepper - half a pound of lump sugar - 2lb of white sugar and 8lb of black sugar, and other spices in abundance.

To two carpenters covering the dormitory, for a month, 13s 2d.

Two bundles of steel containing 66 rods, 14d. Ten stone of iron of Spain, at 7d. per stone, 5s. 10d. Eighteen stone of Weardale iron at 4d. per stone, 5s. 5d.

Beer for the table of the monks for a year, 23s. 10d.

To the tailor for making seven pairs of breeches for the monks, 7d.

Divers medicinal spices bought for the Prior, 5s.

Seven chaldrons of salt, 7,800 red herring, 198 kelinges and codlinges, £16 13s. 6d.

Fourteen capons and eight geese, bought for stocking the manor of Fenham, 3s. 9d.

A table-cloth, with towels, bought for the table of the Prior and Brethren, 17s.

To minstrels of our courtesy during the period of this account, 18d.

A barrel of tar bought for the sheep, with the labour of the man greasing them for 6 days, 7s.

For the labour of the mason working at the bakehouse, which required to be built anew, 7 weeks and three days at 16½d. per week, 10s. 1½d.

The pension paid to the scholars studying at Oxford, 40s.

For painting the image of St Cuthbert, 53s. 4d.

For building a ship and a boat, £17 11s.

A contribution of the Pope and Legatees, £9 13s. 4d.

Paid for an iron chimney, 12s. 10d.

A contribution made to our Lord the King, 30s.

For wine given to the Lord Prior and Monks at Durham, 26s. 6d.

A sloop bought of a certain Scotchman, with the oysters and other goods contained in it, 100s.

Two beds with testers, and four blankets, 33s.

Wines, spices and wax, for the use of the church, and the solace of strangers, 23s. 3d.

Expenses of the Prior to the fair at Darlington, 26s. 2d.

A brazen cauldron bought for the kitchen, 10s.

Six herring nets, 107s. 8d.

Given to the minstrels of divers Lords, 6s. 8d.

Besides income and expenditure there are regular inventories of the things which belonged to the Priory. For the year 1367 we have the following meagre list of books in the Library: "Two illuminated missals, one quarto containing the rule and regulations of St Benedict. Two small red books. The book of St Cuthbert which fell into the sea; one book of sentences belonging to the priory of Coldingam; many pamphlets on divers subjects". This is followed by a lengthy list of the robes and vestments which constitute an important part of every inventory.

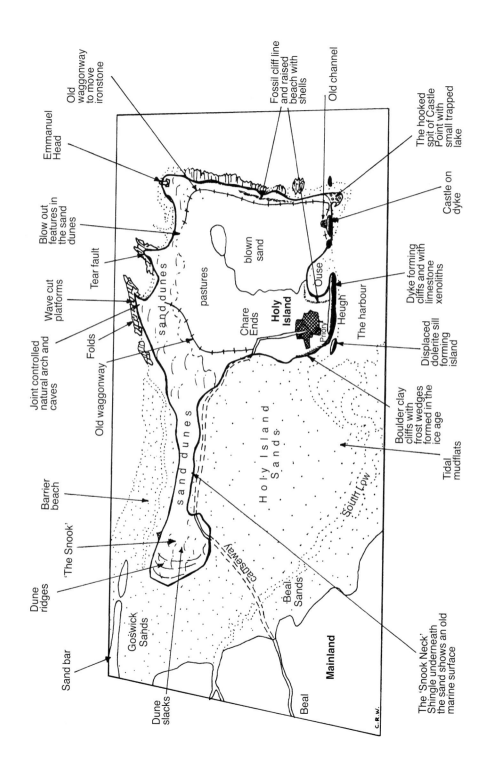

Old waggonway to move ironstone

Emmanuel Head

Fossil cliff line and raised beach with shells

Old channel

The hooked Spit of Castle Point with small trapped lake

Castle on dyke

Blow out features in the sand dunes

Tear fault

Wave cut platforms

Folds

Old waggonway

Joint controlled natural arch and caves

sand dunes

pastures

blown sand

Ouse

Chare Ends

Holy Island

Priory

Heugh

The harbour

Dyke forming cliffs and with limestone xenoliths

Displaced dolerite sill forming island

Boulder clay cliffs with frost wedges formed in the ice age

Tidal mudflats

Barrier beach

sand dunes

Holy Island Sands

South Low

Dune ridges

'The Snook'

causeway

The 'Snook Neck' Shingle underneath the sand shows an old marine surface

Sand bar

Goswick Sands

Dune slacks

Beal Sands

Mainland

Beal

C.R.W.

A geological walk around Holy Island

As well as its unique historical appeal, Holy Island offers a great deal of geological interest to the visitor. It has samples of igneous, metamorphic and sedimentary rocks, plus features of coastal erosion and deposition, glacial deposits, and much evidence of sea level changes.

Most of the island is formed from rocks belonging to the Middle Limestone Group of the Lower Carboniferous period, which contains limestone beds (such as the Eelwell and Acre Limestones), sandstones, shales, coal seams and some ironstone deposits. Most of these rock types have been exploited on a small scale in the past, as evidenced by the old quarries, waggonways, jetties and building stones. Igneous rocks outcrop along the southern margin of the island, and there are fine grained quartz bolerites injected nearly vertically through the Middle Limestone Group deposits in the form of a dyke. This resistant rock was weathered into a prominent line of ridges dissected by faults from St Cuthbert's Island via the Heugh (129417) and the Castle rock (136417) to Scar Jockey (142417). The margins of the dyke show a zone of contact metamorphosed sedimentary rocks where the molten material has baked the surrounding 'country rock'. On the northern side of the Heugh some bolerite exposures show fragments of limestone which have been incorporated inside the dyke as xenoliths.

The Heugh is an excellent starting point for a geological walk because it affords excellent views along the dyke and also enables one to see how the main village is sited on an old shoreline now elevated above sea level. The fossil cliffline can be seen near to the herring house, and searching in this area may reveal some shelly raised black deposits.

The footpath from the harbour follows the shore of the Ouse, a cove eroded into soft deposits, and them passes an old jetty at 135417. From there onwards the path traces the line of the Eastern Waggonway once used for transporting ironstone from the north of the island to that jetty. At Castle point (140417) is a fine hooked split caused by longshore drift currents moving beach deposits southwards.

The walk to the navigational beacon of Emmanuel Head follows the line of more fossil cliffs. At the beacon (139436) a small coal seam can be see in the cliffs, above which are two kinds of boulder clay, one red and the other grey, both of which contain a wide variety of ice transported rocks.

The northern shore has two large bays, Sandon Bay and Coves Bay, divided by a fine rocky peninsula called Castle Head (133440) which has a sizeable wave cut platform exposed at low tide. A tear fault affects Coves Bay and creates a shatter zone along which the sea has eroded an inlet. It is in this area that much of the ironstone was formerly worked. At Snipe Point (126438) there is a natural arch controlled by the pattern of jointing, together with several interesting caves. The foreshore just west of here reveals a series of upfolds (anticlines), some of which bring limestone to the surface which becomes dissolved by the seawater along the joints to create a limestone pavement of clints and grykes.

It is believed that the Snook (100435) was once separated from the rest of Holy Island though it is now joined by a sandy neck which forms part of a large blown sand ridge that includes the Links (125435). These dunes have many irregular hollows called 'blow outs' which show that the dunes are still unstable. From the Links it is possible to return via Chare Ends to the village along the line of the former Western Waggonway. [*This geological section and the map are by C.R. Warn.*]

Maps, Sea Charts and Navigation Beacons

The first map of Holy Island appeared in Speede's atlas in the year 1610 [see page 1]. It was copied by the Dutch cartographer Blaeu with the title Insula Sacra; vulgo Holy Island et Farne, in his world atlas issued in 1645. Many English map makers, for example Morden in 1695, included maps of the island in their atlases.

The first sea chart of Holy Island was published in 1693 by Captain Greenville Collins in his famous sea atlas entitled Great Britain's Coasting Pilot. The sea chart opposite was published in 1798 by William Heather.

The two obelisks on the mainland south of The Heugh are navigation beacons. Sailors entering the harbour from any direction align the two beacons and when one obscures the other a new course is set by aligning the navigation mast on The Heugh with the bell tower on St Mary's Church.

Holy Island – a short history and guide by Frank Graham. This edition 2005
ISBN 0946928134   © 1987 Butler Publishing, Throlton, Morpeth, Northumberland NE65 7LP
Originally published by Frank Graham. Published by Butler Publishing in 1987
Printed by Studio Three, Washington NE38 8QA

front cover – top Incipit page to St Mark's Gospel, from the *Lindisfarne Gospels*, c.700. Reproduction is by permission of the British Library (c2176-04, shelfmark: Cotton Nero D. IV)
front cover – bottom Holy Island Fisherman, c.1850. From an original painting by Ronald Embleton. Reproduction is by permission of Frank Graham.
back cover – top Carpet page, introducing St Matthew's Gospel, from the *Lindisfarne Gospels*. Reproduction is by permission of the British Library (c2176-05, shelfmark: Cotton Nero D. IV)
back cover – bottom Lindisfarne Priory. From an original painting by Ronald Embleton based on a reconstruction by R. Neville Hadcock. Reproduction is by permission of Frank Graham.